ANIMAL ANALOGUES

LECTOR HOUSE PUBLIC DOMAIN WORKS

This book is a result of an effort made by Lector House towards making a contribution to the preservation and repair of original classic literature. The original text is in the public domain in the United States of America, and possibly other countries depending upon their specific copyright laws.

In an attempt to preserve, improve and recreate the original content, certain conventional norms with regard to typographical mistakes, hyphenations, punctuations and/or other related subject matters, have been corrected upon our consideration. However, few such imperfections might not have been rectified as they were inherited and preserved from the original content to maintain the authenticity and construct, relevant to the work. The work might contain a few prior copyright references which have been retained, wherever considered relevant to the part of the construct. We believe that this work holds historical, cultural and/or intellectual importance in the literary works community, therefore despite the oddities, we accounted the work for print as a part of our continuing effort towards preservation of literary work and our contribution towards the development of the society as a whole, driven by our beliefs.

We are grateful to our readers for putting their faith in us and accepting our imperfections with regard to preservation of the historical content. We shall strive hard to meet up to the expectations to improve further to provide an enriching reading experience.

Though, we conduct extensive research in ascertaining the status of copyright before redeveloping a version of the content, in rare cases, a classic work might be incorrectly marked as not-in-copyright. In such cases, if you are the copyright holder, then kindly contact us or write to us, and we shall get back to you with an immediate course of action.

HAPPY READING!

ANIMAL ANALOGUES

ROBERT WILLIAMS WOOD

ISBN: 978-93-5420-155-4

Published: -

LECTOR HOUSE LLP
E-MAIL: lectorpublishing@gmail.com

ANIMAL ANALOGUES.
VERSES AND ILLUSTRATIONS

BY

ROBERT WILLIAMS WOOD.

Author of "How To Tell The Birds From the Flowers."

CONTENTS

THE BEE. THE BEET. THE BEETLE.

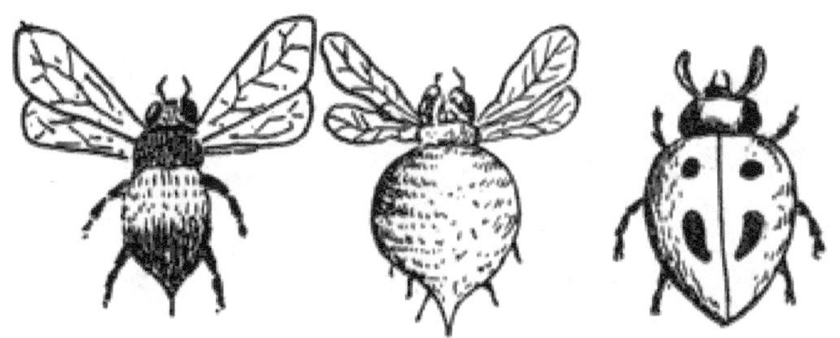

Good Mr. Darwin once contended
That Beetles were from Bees descended;
And as my pictures show, I think,
The Beet must be the missing-link.
The Sugar-Beet and Honey-Bee
Supply the Beetle's pedigree:
The family is now complete, —
The Bee, the Beetle and the Beet.

THE ANT. THE PHEAS-ANT.

The Ant is known by his ant-ennae,
Where-as the pheas-ant hasn't any,
And that is why he wears, instead,
A small red cap upon his head:
Without his Fez, indeed the pheasant
Would be quite bald and quite un-Pleasant.

THE BUNNY. THE TUNNY.

The superficial naturalists have often been misled,
By failing to dis-crim-inate between the tail and head:
It really is unfortunate such carelessness prevails,
Because the Bunnies have their heads where Tunnies have their tails.

THE EEL. THE ELEPHANT.

The marked aversion which we feel,
When in the presence of the Eel,
Makes many view with consternation,
The Elephant's front ele-vation.
Such folly must be clearly due
To their peculiar point of view.

THE PUSS. THE OCTO-PUS.

The Octo-pus or Cuttle-fish!
I'm sure that none of us would wish
To have him scuttle 'round the house,
Like puss, when she espies a mouse:
When you secure your house-hold pet,
Be very sure you do not get
The Octo-pus, or there may be
Dom-es-tic in-felis-ity.

THE GNU. THE NEWT.

The Gnu conspicuously wears
His coat of gnumerous bristling hairs,
While, as we see, the modest Newt
Of such a coat is destitute.
(I'm only telling this to you,
And it is strictly "entre gnu".)
In point of fact the Newt is nude,
And therefore he does not obtrude,
But hides in some secluded gnook,
Beneath the surface of the brook:
It's almost more than he can bear,
To slyly take his breath of air,
His need of which is absolute,
Because, you see, he is a Pneu-t.*

*This stands for air, like aero-static,
Greek—"pneumos"—air—comp-air "pneu-matic".

THE HARE. THE HARRIER.

The Harrier, harassed by the Hare,
Presents a picture of despair;
Altho' as far as I'm concerned,
I love to see the tables turned.
The Harrier flies with all his might,
It is a harum-scare'm flight:
I'm not surprised he does not care
To meet the fierce pursuing Hare!

THE PIPE-FISH. THE SEA-GAR.

To smoke a herring is to make
A most lamentable mistake,
Particularly since there are
The Pipe-fish and the long Sea-gar:
Bear this in mind when next you wish
To smoke your after-dinner fish.

THE COW. THE COWRY.

The Cowry seems to be, somehow,
A sort of mouth-piece for the Cow:
A speaking likeness one might say,
Which I've endeavored to portray.

THE DOE. THE DODO.

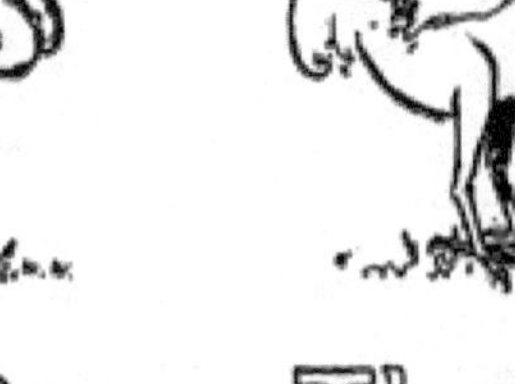

The Doe and her peculiar double
No longer are a source of trouble,
Because the Dodo, it appears,
Has been extinct for many years.
She was too proud to disembark
With total strangers in Noah's Ark,
And we rejoice because her pride
Our Nature book has simplified.

THE RAY. THE RAVEN.

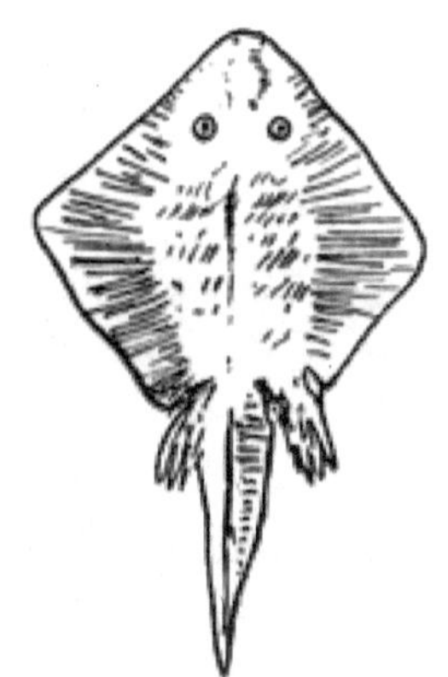 

The Raven is a kind of crow,
Immortalized by Mr. Poe,
And we are often led astray
By its resemblance to the Ray;
The one which I denominate,
Is termed by fisher-men the Skate;
I much prefer the latter phrase,
There are so many kinds of Rays:
There're Rays of hope, and Rays of light.
X Rays, and Rays more re-con-dite,
Which, though of interest to Science,
With Ravens have but small alliance.

THE COOT. THE BANDICOOT.

I do not wish to at-tri-bute
Importance to the common Coot,
Or mud-hen, whom most persons scorn,
Because she chanced to be "Earth-born".
The small Australian Bandicoots
Are said to spring from Kanga-roots,
Which roots, as you of course foresee,
Are those of their ancestral tree,
The motto of which vegetable
Is just "O possum"*(I am able).

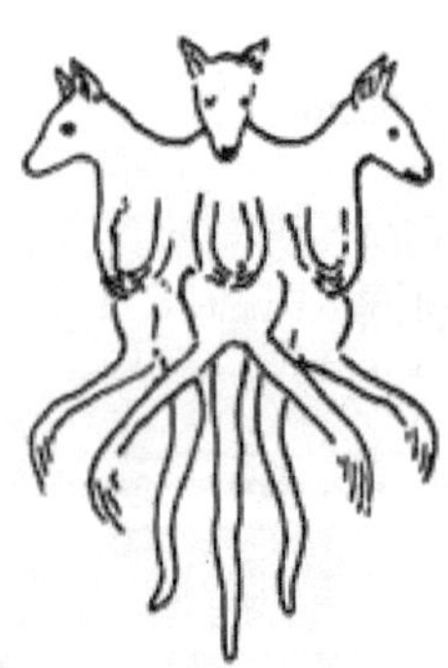

*The Bandicoot and Kangaroo,
As well as the Opossum too,
Are relatives because all three
Belong to the same family.

THE APE. THE GRAPE.

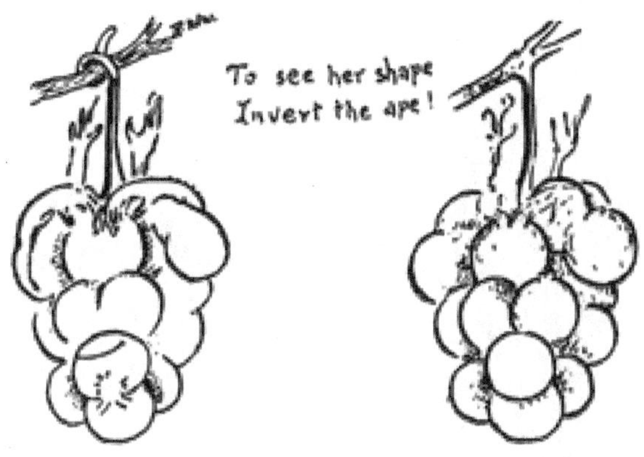

The Apes, from whom we are descended,
Hang ape-x down from trees suspended,
And since we find them in the trees,
We term them arbor-iginees.
We all have seen the monkey-shines,
Cut up by those who pluck from vines
The Grape and then subject its juices
To Baccha-nalian abuses.

THE ELK. THE WHELK.

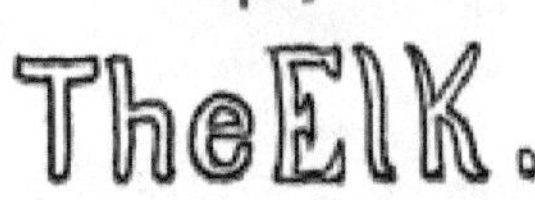

A roar of welkome through the welkin
Is certain proof you'll find the Elk "in";
But if you listen to the shell,
In which the Whelk is said to dwell,
And hear a roar, beyond a doubt
It indicates the Whelk is "out".

CROSS BILL. SWEET WILLIAM.

No-body but an imbecile
Mistakes Sweet William for Cross Bill;
And even I can scarcely claim
The skill to make them look the same,
Which proves there's nothing in a name.

THE PITCHER PLANT. THE FLY-CATCHER.

The Pitcher Plant we may define,
The flower of the base-ball nine;
This name perhaps the plant belies,
For Pitcher Plants sometimes catch flies;
The "Fly"-Catcher we educate
To firmly stand behind the plate,
To stop, and treat with circumspection,
Whatever comes in his direction.

THE ANTELOPE. THE CANTELOPE.

The Antelope and Cantelope
Lie side by side upon the slope,
And careless persons might, I fear,
Mistake the melon for the deer.
If you will tap the Cantelope, reposing on the ground,
It does not move, but just emits a melon-choly sound;
But should you try, however, to apply a stethoscope,
And attempt this auscultation on the antlered Antelope,
And should see an imitation of a very rapid flight,
And should say, "It is the Antelope!" I think you would be right.

THE P-COCK. THE Q-CUMBER.

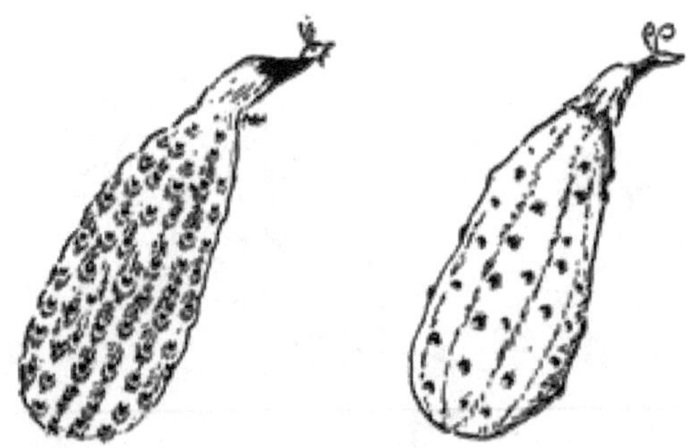

The striking similarity of this P-Q-liar pair,
No longer need en-cumber us or fill us with despair;
The P-Cock and the Q-Cumber you never need confuse.
If you pay attention to the I's and mind your P's and Q's.

THE PEN-GUIN. THE SWORD-FISH.

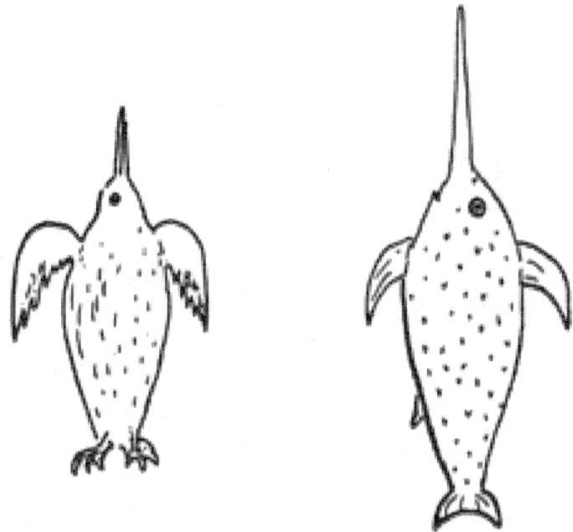

We have for many years been bored
By that old saw about the sword
And pen, and now we all rejoice,
To see how Nature made her choice:
She made, regardless of offendin’,
The Sword-fish mightier than the Penguin.

THE YELLOW-HAMMER. THE SAW-FISH.

The Yellow-Hammer, or the Flicker,
More briefly "Golden-winged Wood-picker",
My drawing of which striking bird
May seem to you perhaps absurd,
You even may suspect I stole
The idea from some Totem-pole:
But when you gaze upon the Fish,
You lose all patience and say "Pish!
I don't believe you ever saw
A Saw-fish look like this, Oh Pshaw!
There certainly is some mistake,
This is a saw-did Nature fake,
In fact a perfect cata-clysm
Of fishy Yellow-journalism."

THE PANSY. THE CHIM-PANSY.

Observe how Nature's necromancies
Have clearly painted on the Pansies
These almost human counte-nances,
In yellow, blue and black nu-ances.
The face, however, seems to me
To be that of the Chimpanzee,
A fact which makes the gentle Pansy
Appeal no longer to my fancy.

NAUGHT. NAUTILUS.

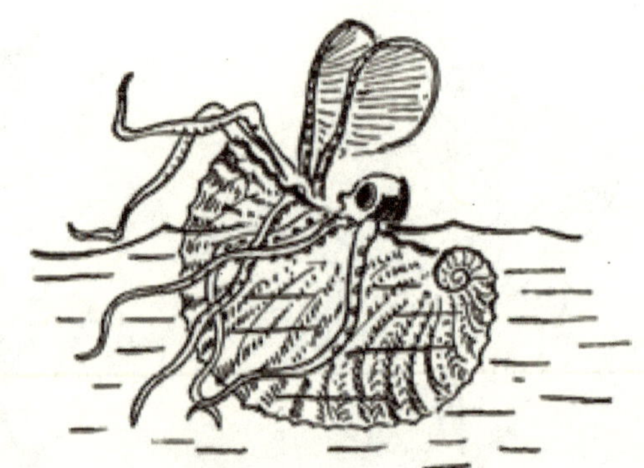

The Argonaut or Nautilus,
With habits quite adventurous,
A combination of a snail,
A jelly-fish and paper sail.
The parts of him that did not jell
Are packed securely in his shell.
It is not strange that when I sought
To find his double, I found naught.

AUTHOR'S ADD-END-'EM.

If you have read my former words,
And learned to recognize the Birds,
And how to tell them from Flowers,
And know these Analogues of ours,
You never need be led astray
By Darwin, Audubon, or Gray,
Whose writings, though considered classic,
Savor some-what of the Jurassic.
Your work though is but just begun,
While mine, I'm glad to say, is done.
To you the field I now leave clear,
Upset my ink, and disappear!

Lector House believes that a society develops through a two-fold approach of continuous learning and adaptation, which is derived from the study of classic literary works spread across the historic timeline of literature records. Therefore, we aim at reviving, repairing and redeveloping all those inaccessible or damaged but historically as well as culturally important literature across subjects so that the future generations may have an opportunity to study and learn from past works to embark upon a journey of creating a better future.

This book is a result of an effort made by Lector House towards making a contribution to the preservation and repair of original ancient works which might hold historical significance to the approach of continuous learning across subjects.

HAPPY READING & LEARNING!

LECTOR HOUSE LLP
E-MAIL: lectorpublishing@gmail.com